CLAIM OF C. P. VAN NESS.

WASHINGTON CITY, *February* 16, 1846.

To the honorable the Senate and House of Representatives of the United States, in Congress assembled:

C. P. Van Ness, of the city of New York, begs leave, respectfully, to make the following representation and application—

That he was Collector of the Customs for the District of Vermont, from the 15th day of February, 1813, to the 1st of February, 1818.

That during the years 1813 and 1814 he seized certain quantities of merchandise which had been introduced from the British Province of Lower Canada, in violation of the non-importation acts of Congress then in force, by which the said merchandise had become forfeited to the United States, and the proceeds of which were distributable agreeably to the provisions of the 91st section of the act regulating the collection of duties, passed on the 2d day of March, 1799.

That the said quantities of merchandise were duly proceeded against in the District Court of the United States for the Vermont District, and were, by order of the said Court, delivered to the claimants thereof on bonds, in conformity with the provisions of the 89th section of the act above referred to, for the collection of duties.

That during the pendency of the suits or prosecutions, and between the years 1814 and 1820, the forfeitures incurred in the said cases, respectively, were remitted by the honorable Secretary of the Treasury of the United States, upon payment of the costs which had accrued, and reserving an amount, in each case, equal to what the duties would have been on a legal importation.

That the sums thus reserved were treated at the Treasury Department as *duties*, and required to be accounted for in the same manner as if they had accrued on legal importations, and they were accordingly paid into the Treasury.

That in the year 1834, and while this petitioner was absent from his country, it was unanimously decided by the Supreme Court, in the case of McLane against the United States, which is to be found in the 6th volume of Peters's Reports, at page 404, and which originated in a seizure made in the year 1812, by Mr. M'Lane, as Collector of Delaware, for a violation of the same laws under which the seizures of the petitioner were made, that the reservation in the remission of that forfeiture (which was precisely like the reservations in the cases of the petitioner) was of a portion of the *forfeiture*, and could not be considered as *duties*, since no duties *could* accrue from the introduction of prohibited goods; and that, therefore, the sum thus reserved was distributable in like manner as if the whole forfeiture had been exacted.

That on the return of this petitioner to the United States, which was in the year 1839, he discovered that it had been thus solemnly and conclusively settled that a moiety of the sums reserved in the remissions of the forfeitures incurred within his district, and paid into the Treasury, as already stated, belonged to himself; there having been no naval officer or surveyor within the district at the time referred to.

That, upon this, he would at once have presented his claim for the sums belonging to him, had he not then had unsettled accounts with the Government, which he did not wish to mix up with any other matters, and which he was determined honorably to close without the aid of this claim.

That soon after the final close of those accounts, and when he was about to bring forward this matter, he was appointed Collector of the Customs for the Port of New York, in which office he served about one year, ending on the first day of July last.

That while the facts contained in this statement furnish, as the petitioner believes, sufficient reasons for the delay in the presentation of this claim to the proper branch of the Government, it may, at the same time, be proper to state, that such delay can produce no injury or inconvenience to the Uniied States, since all the accounts of the petitioner, as Collector of Vermont, are now to be found in the Treasury Department; and by these accounts the amount of the money in question (a moiety of which is about $17,000) can be ascertained with the same facility, and the same certainty, that it could have been at any moment since the payments took place.

The petitioner would, respectfully, add, that on leaving the office of Collector of New York, he might have retained in his hands an amount of public money equal to the sum now claimed by him; and, in case of a suit by the United States, have pleaded the said sum in offset, since the law applicable to the case had been settled by the same Court before which such suit might ultimately have come; but that he was unwilling to withhold from the Government any money which was not freely admitted to be his due, and could not be regularly allowed to him by the accounting officers; and that, therefore, he faithfully accounted for, and paid over, all the public moneys which had come into his hands.

Wherefore the petitioner prays that Congress, upon consideration of all the facts and circumstances of his case, will pass a law directing the officers of the Treasury Department to pay him such sums of money, with the interest thereon, as may be found, upon the principles above set forth, to have legally belonged to him at the time of their payment into the Treasury.

All which is most respectfully submitted by,

C. P. VAN NESS.

WASHINGTON, *January* 16, 1847.

SIR: Having been informed that a petition preferred by me to Congress, for the payment of certain moneys claimed by me from the United States, has been referred to the Treasury Department for a report, I beg leave to present the following communication in relation to the case:

The particular character of my claim it will not be necessary here to describe, since that is fully set forth in my petition. But a detailed statement of the amounts paid into the Treasury, and of which I claim the return of a moiety, is herewith sent to you.

It will be found that all the accounts rendered by me while Collector of the Vermont district are now in the Treasury Department, with the single exception of the detailed bond accounts, which appear to have been mislaid or lost. Of these latter I now send fair and complete duplicates, verified by the oath of the person who made them, as well as those forwarded to the Treasury Department, at or about the time they bear date. These duplicates can, also, all of them, be verified by the balances of bonds of the corresponding quarters stated in my general quarterly accounts, which are in the Department.

I also send copies and extracts from the records of the United States District Court in Vermont, duly authenticated, showing that all the moneys in question accrued in cases where merchandise had been unlawfully imported from the British Province of Lower Canada, during the years 1813 and 1814, and had been seized and libelled as forfeited to the United States, and where the penalties and forfeitures were remitted by the Secretary of the Treasury, with the exception, or reservation, (besides costs and charges of prosecutions,) of those portions constituting the said moneys.

The above mentioned papers and documents will, as I conceive, fully establish the facts upon which I have founded my claim. But I have to ask that, in setting forth those facts in the report to be made by the Department, the additional fact will be stated, that the accounts of Col. McLane, the former Collector of Delaware, and in whose case the Supreme Court made the decision referred to in my petition, were finally adjusted at the Treasury upon the principles established by that decision.

I have the honor to remain, respectfully, your obedient servant,

C. P. VAN NESS.

J. W. McCulloh, Esq.,
Comptroller.

Treasury Department,
Comptroller's Office, February 15, 1847.

Sir: The petition of C. P. Van Ness, Esq., formerly Collector of the Customs in the district of Vermont, that was transmitted to this office by the Hon. Chester Ashley, by instructions from the Judiciary Committee, with the request that you would furnish any information on file relating to its subject matter, to wit: his claim to receive a moiety of the money collected in the said district, and paid into the Treasury as duties on goods the importation whereof was prohibited, amounting, with interest that accrued thereon, in the aggregate, to the sum of $36,353, having been referred to this office, I have the honor to return the same with a letter that was addressed to me by said petitioner on the 16th ultimo, submitting the enclosed papers, therein referred to as extracts from the records of the U. S. District Court for the District aforesaid, lettered D, E, F, which show that the forfeiture of said goods was remitted by the Secretary of the Treasury, upon the payment of the costs of suit, and duties with interest thereupon, and a statement of moneys that were collected and paid into the Treasury of the United States, as duties on the prohibited goods mentioned in said extract, with the interest that accrued thereon, lettering G, shewing the aggregate sum of money that was so received and paid into the Treasury of the U. S. amounted to $36,353, accompanied by a joint report which I caused Messrs. McCorkle and North, accountants in this office, to make of the result of their examination of said extracts and statement, and from which it appears that the petitioner has correctly stated the circumstances, law, and amount of his claim ; and perhaps I should further remark that their examination has been made by referring for particulars to original quarterly accounts that were duly rendered to this Department, except the detailed accounts of the bonds taken for duties, the original of these having either been mislaid or destroyed by the conflagration of the Treasury; but as their loss has been compensated by the delivery of duplicates of said bond accounts that were prepared at the time when said originals were respectively transmitted to this Department, the examination of said accounts may be considered as accurate as if it had been made with reference to said originals, as it appears from quarterly accounts of the customs, that were duly rendered by Collectors Van Ness and Fisk, and settled at this Department, that the sum of the aforesaid duty bonds, with the interest that accrued thereon, has been collected and paid into the Treasury of the United States.

With great respect, your obedient servant,

J. W. McCULLOH,
Comptroller.

Hon. R. J. Walker,
Secretary of the Treasury.

Comptroller's Office,
February 9, 1847.

Sir: We have examined the accounts of Cornelius P. Van Ness and James Fisk, former Collectors of the Customs for the District of Vermont, and the accompanying certified extracts from the records of the U. S. District Court for said District, marked D, E, F, verified by our initials; and find therefrom that certain goods were imported into said District, in violation of the non-intercourse and non-importation laws, between the first of February 1813, and the 27th of August, 1814, by persons residing in the United States; that they were seized and libelled by C. P. Van Ness, then Collector; that they were surrendered to the claimants by order of the Court, after they had given bonds for the duties, upon their executing bonds, with condition to pay the appraised value of the goods, if the forfeiture thereof should be decreed; that the Secretary of the Treasury subsequently remitted said forfeiture upon condition that the costs of said libel suits and the sum of said duties should be paid; and that the claimants paid said costs, and the sum of $31,527 94 as duties, which with $4,825 91 that had accrued as interest thereon amounted per accompanying statement marked G, verified by our initials, to the aggregate sum of $36,353 85, which was received and has been retained by the United States, notwithstanding it has been settled by their Supreme Court, in the case of Allen McLane, former Collector for the Districts of Delaware, (vide 6th volume of Peters' Reports, page 404,) that moneys received into the Treasury and retained as duties on goods, the importation whereof was prohibited, should be considered as penalty reserved, and be distributed accordingly, since duties accrue only on goods which may be lawfully imported, and not upon goods the importation whereof is prohibited under penalty of forfeiture for the mere act of importation, and the fact that after said decision was made the accounts of said Collector McLane were adjusted at the Treasury in conformity with the principles thereby established, and which seem to be equally applicable to the claim of late Collector Van Ness.

Respectfully submitted,

J. K. McCORKLE,
J. BARTRAM NORTH.

To J. W. McCulloh, Esq.,
Comptroller of the Treasury.

Treasury Department,
Comptroller's Office, November 24, 1849.

Sir: The petition of the Hon. C. P. Van Ness, of the city of New York, was presented on the 19th day of February, 1846, to the Senate, and referred to the Committee on the Judiciary.

It states that he was Collector of Customs for the District of Vermont from the 15th day of February, 1813, to the 1st of February, 1818; that in the years 1813 and 1814, he seized a large quantity of merchandise from time to time, which was forfeited to the United States; that the goods he seized were proceeded against in the United States District Court, and by order of said Court were bonded and delivered to the claimants under the 89th section of the act of March 2d, 1799; that the forfeitures were remitted by the Secretary of the Treasury, from 1814 to 1820, on the payment, costs, and what would have been the duties on legal importations; and he claimed one moiety, or about $17,000, of said payments, as forfeitures agreeably to the 91st section of the act regulating the collection of duties, passed on the 2d day of March, 1799.

In support of his claim, he contends it is similar to the claim of the late Allen McLane, collector in Deleware, which was decided in his favor in 1832 by the Supreme Court of the United States. He explains the omission to present his claim earlier in not knowing his legal rights before the decision in 1832, and at that time he was abroad in the service of the United States, and did not return until 1839; that he wished to settle his account without reference to this claim; that soon after said settlement he was appointed Collector of New York, and remained in that office until July, 1845.

Mr. Ashley, chairman of the said Judiciary Committee, on the 8th of January, 1847, (incorrectly dated 1846,) referred the petition to the Secretary of the Treasury, with a request that he furnish the Committee with the evidence on file in relation to the matter therein set forth, together with the action of the Government in other similar cases, and such observations as he might deem proper.

This letter and petition were referred by the Secretary to the 1st Comptroller on the 11th of January, 1847. Mr. McCulloh, having caused an investigation to be made on the 15th day of February, 1847, reported certain facts to the Secretary of the Treasury, accompanied by some papers, in answer to the requirements of the Committee.

This report was not satisfactory to the Secretary of the Treasury, and on the 20th of the same month, he returned the petition to the Comptroller; and after mentioning what had taken place, and the importance of the question involved, he said, "I therefore return all the papers to you, and request an official report showing what evidence remains in the files of this Department, not only in regard to this claim, but other similar cases, together with the action of the Government thereon. You will be pleased to state in your report the amount that will probably be required to provide for all claims which may be established upon the principles set forth in the petition of Mr. Van Ness, and furnish such explanations and observations as shall enable Congress to act with full knowledge of the consequences. This claim appears to have arisen more than thirty years since, and has been presented for the first time at the present Congress. After such a delay, when so many documents and papers which might throw light upon the subject have been destroyed, much research and information will doubtless be necessary to fulfill the views of the Committee in regard to similar cases. I desire a thorough examination and full report on the subject, embracing the foregoing considerations as to the consequences of establishing the principles upon which Mr. Van Ness's claim is founded."

I understand a clerk was sent to obtain information at the custom houses in the Middle, Eastern and Northern States in regard to the amount of forfeitures remitted, or bonds cancelled, which were given for goods delivered to claimants after seizure, where the condition of remission was the payment of costs and charges and duties, or either of them, or otherwise, and the amount of duties that were paid on such conditional remissions; and, so far as such information was obtained, it is contained in various papers, which are on file in the office of the Commissioner of Customs, and which the Commissioner has temporarily placed in my hands. No other report was made by my predecessor, and the examination is resumed at the request of Mr. Van Ness and under your verbal instructions.

The commencement of Mr. Van Ness's term, as Collector in Vermont, was on the 15th of February, 1813, as he states in his petition, but its termination is a subject of some doubt.

Inasmuch as he asks for a moiety of the duties paid on the goods that were seized, on which was a remission of fines or forfeitures, and inasmuch as such remission extended through several years, it may be of importance to know where his services ended.

This view is strengthened from the consideration that, if Congress should grant relief, there should be deducted from the moiety of duties paid into the Treasury such sums as he has received as commissions on such money as may be refunded. The President nominated Cornelius P. Van Ness one of the Commissioners on the part of the United States, in March, 1816, in compliance with the 5th article of the treaty of Ghent, concluded between the United States and Great Britain on the 24th of December, 1814, and the Senate confirmed this nomination on the 3d of April following.

It appears from the settlement of his account, on the 9th of July, 1823, that his salary as such Commisssioner commenced on the said 3d of April, and continued to the 31st of December, 1820, at the rate of $4,444 44 per annum, amounting to $21,086 67
And from thence to the 13th of April, 1822, at $2,500 per annum, amounting to 3,214 28

$24,300 95

James Fish was appointed Collector by the President in the same district on the 11th of November, 1817, and he was appointed permanently on the 29th of December, 1817. I cannot find his oath of office nor its date, nor the time when he entered upon the duties of his office. The quarterly returns indicate that Mr. Van Ness continued to be Collector to the close of the 4th quarter 1817, and some of the correspondence speaks of his being Collector after that. It is supposed that the original accounts and vouchers of Mr. Van Ness, as collector, were destroyed by the fire which consumed the Treasury building; but there are accounts which purport to be applicable to that period of time, which it is said were furnished by Mr. Van Ness, as duplicates, since the petition was presented to Congress. The forfeitures under the seizures made on the northern frontier in 1813 and 1814, when Mr. Van Ness was Collector, were incurred under and by virtue of the non-intercourse acts of March 1, 1809; May 1, 1810; March 2, 1811.

By the acts of 1st of March, 1809, and 1st May, 1810, power was conferred on the Secretary of the Treasury to remit fines, penalties, and forfeitures, when application should be made as required by an act approved March 3, 1797, which was:

Sec. 1. That whenever any person or persons who shall have incurred any fine, penalty, forfeiture, or disability, or shall have been interested in any vessel, goods, wares, or merchandise, which shall have been subject to any seizure, forfeiture, or disability, by force of any present or future law of the United States, &c., "stating that the cases shall prefer his petition to the Judge of the district in which such fine, penalty, forfeiture, or disability shall have accrued, truly and particularly setting forth the circumstances of his case; and shall pray that the same may be mitigated or remitted, into the circumstances of the case, first causing reasonable notice to be given to the person or persons claiming such fine, penalty, or forfeiture, and to the Attorney of the United States for such district, that may have an opportunity of showing cause against the mitigation or remission thereof; and shall cause the facts which shall appear upon such to be stated and annexed to the petition, and direct their transmission to the Secretary of the Treasury of the United States, who shall thereupon have power to mitigate or remit such fine, forfeiture, or penalty, or remove such disability, or any part thereof, if, in his opinion, the same shall have been incurred without wilful negligence or any intention of fraud in the person or persons incurring the same, and to direct the prosecution, if any shall have been instituted for the recovery thereof, to cease, and be discontinued, upon such terms or conditions as he may deem reasonable and just."

The duration of this act was limited to two years, but was made perpetual by an act approved 11th of February, 1800.

The power to remit was without any restriction, except in the case of "*wilful negligence* and *intention* to *defraud*."

The non-intercourse acts of March 1, 1809, May 1, 1810, and March 2, 1811, prohibited the importation of goods, wares, and merchandise from England and France, and their colonies and dependencies, and they interdicted all commercial intercourse with those powers under certain circumstances, and for certain designated periods. The Congress of the United States declared war against Great Britain on the 18th June, 1812. The non-intercourse and the embargo acts had prevented the importation of goods from the countries most extensively engaged in manufactures, and the demand had not been supplied by factories in this country; and when the industry of the people had made them generally comfortable, there were not sufficient blankets, nor woollen clothes, to supply the army. Our merchants, during the restrictions mentioned, had made purchases in foreign countries before the declaration of war, and principally of the British, in anticipation that friendly relations would be restored with Great Britain and France; and that those first in the market would realize the greatest profits. Complaints were made that the restrictive measures of the Government were ruinous to their pecuniary concerns. The wants of the people, the destitution of the army, with the hope of great gain, were strong inducements for violating the laws of the United States by the clandestine introduction into the United States of the goods and merchandise thus purchased, principally through Canada and by the way of Lake Champlain. The Courts so construed the revenue laws, irrespective of the non-intercourse acts, as to permit the goods which were seized to be delivered to the claimants on the execution of bonds that the goods should be returned if condemned, or the penalty of the bonds to be paid if the conditions were not executed. It was under the circumstances, and at a period when the means for carrying on the war were exceedingly limited, that the act of 27th February, 1813, was passed, which indirectly opened the ports to foreign importations.

The 1st section enacts:

"That in all cases where goods, wares, and merchandise have been imported or introduced into the United States (the same not having been clandestinely imported or introduced) from the dependencies of the United Kingdom of Great Britain and Ireland, since the declaration of war by the United States against the said Kingdon, or which were shipped from the said Kingdom prior to the second of February, one thousand eight hundred and eleven, whereby the person or persons interested in such goods, wares, or merchandise, or concerned in any importation or introduction thereof into the United States, hath or have incurred any fine, penalty, or forfeiture, under an act entitled 'An act concerning the commercial intercourse between the United States and Great Britain and France and their dependencies, and for other purposes,' and the act supplementary to the act last mentioned; on such person or persons petitioning for relief to any Judge or Court, proper to hear the same, in pursuance of the provisions of the act entitled 'An act to provide for mitigating or remitting the forfeitures, penalties, and disabilities accruing in certain cases therein mentioned;' and on the facts being shown, on inquiry had by said Judge or Court, stated and transmitted, as by the said act is required, to the Secretary of the Treasury, in all such cases wherein it shall be proved to his satisfaction that the said goods, wares, and merchandise, at the time of their importation or introduction into the United States, were *bona fide* American property, that they were not clandestinely imported or introduced, and that they were imported or introduced since the declaration of war aforesaid, the Secretary of the Treasury is hereby directed to remit all fines, penalties, and forfeitures that may have been incurred under the said acts, in consequence of such importation or introduction into the United States, upon the costs and charges that have arisen, or may arise, and on payment of the duties that would have been payable by law on such goods, wares, and merchandise, if legally imported, and also to direct the prosecution or prosecutions, if any shall have been instituted, for the recovery of the said fines, penalties, and forfeitures, to cease, and to be discontinued.'

The phraseology of the act in the word "introduced," in connexion with the word "imported," is peculiar to this act, (so far as examination has been made,) and most probably was inserted to apply to the goods, wares, and merchandise brought into the United States from the adjoining British Provinces.

The Secretary of the Treasury and the Courts of the United States construed this act prospectively, as well as to the transactions before its date; and the duties remitted during the time Mr. Van Ness was in office were by virtue of its provisions, so far as the northern frontier was concerned.

By the act of 3d of March, 1797, the power to remit fines, &c., was confined to cases devoid of "Wilful negligence, or any intention of fraud," and by the act of the 27th of February, 1813, it was confined to cases, where the goods, &c., were imported or introduced from Great Britain, &c.

1st. Where the goods, &c., at the time of importation or introduction were American property.

2d. Not clandestinely imported or introduced.

3d. Imported or introduced since the declaration of war.

The proceedings to bring the cases for relief before the Secretary of the Treasury were to be under the act of March 3, 1797, and it is to be borne in mind that notice was to be given to the person or persons claiming such fine, &c., and to the Attorney of the United States, that each might have an opportunity of showing cause against the remission thereof.

It is not alleged by Mr. Van Ness in these cases that he was not notified, and it is not to be presumed that he did not know of the proceedings before the Judge, for the purpose of, and preparatory to, asking the Secretary of the Treasury to remit the fines, penalties, and forfeitures. The act of February 27, 1813, did in effect legalize the importation or introduced of goods, &c., which were imported or introduced openly, after the declaration of war, and were of American property. They must have necessarily been seized, (which was only formal,) that legal proceedings might be had for the purpose of enabling the Judge of the proper district to take and report testimony to the Secretary of the Treasury on the three points mentioned, and without such report the Secretary could not make any examination to ascertain whether the petitioner was entitled to relief or not. The great expense on the northern lines during that period was not to interrupt the regular open importation or introduction of goods which must necessarily go to the custom-house, but to prevent goods, &c., from being imported or introduced clandestinely into the United States, whereby the revenue would have been defrauded.

The remission of the fine on condition of paying the duties and costs, and the consumption of the goods in the country, followed as matters of course.

Mr. Van Ness acquiesced in these proceedings without ascertaining any claims, or pretending he had them.

Among the papers obtained by the agent, who visited the ports of the northeast and north, as mentioned above, is a letter addressed to the 1st Comptroller, Mr. McCulloh, by Mr. Bradbury, Collector in the District of Passamaquoddy, in the State of Maine, dated October 21, 1848.

Most of the custom-house papers were destroyed during the war of 1812, and Mr. Bradbury obtained information from individuals familiar with the history of the war, and from the records in his possession, and from said sources. He says:

"The fact is apparent that large amounts of foreign goods were brought into the United States through this district during the war, and the period of non-importation, and non-intercourse, and embargo, preceding it. Besides the large quantities actually smuggled without detection, there were many cargoes introduced into the district by merchants, who became informers against themselves, for the purpose of receiving the informant's share of the seizure. These goods were seized, appraised, delivered to claimants on bond, and condemned.

"In some instances the forfeiture was remitted on payment of costs, in others on payment of duties. The records of the District Court of Maine should exhibit all these cases; but no other information can be found here, than is contained in the papers marked 2 and 3, herewith transmitted. The precise amount paid in each instance nowhere appears."

Paper marked No. 2 contains a list of ten seizures in the District of Passamaqnoddy, between the 18th of June, 1812, and the 26th of February, 1813—for which petition had been presented to the District Judge for the remission of duties.

Paper marked No. 3 contains a list of 19 seizures within the same period, and in which the same proceedings were had as in the other case.

Copies of the papers are exhibited marked No. 1. The following statement is at the bottom of the paper No. 3:

"Previous to the above, and the within mentioned merchandise being delivered to me, the claimants had called on me at the custom-house, and informed me of their intention to bring the above and within merchandise into the United States, and to deliver the same to me as Collector of the District of Passamaquoddy, and there did not appear (as far as came to my knowledge) the least appearance of a clandestine introduction of the before mentioned goods into the Uhited States.

"L. TRESCOTT,
"*Collector*.

"AUGUST 13, 1813."

A statement substantially the same is annexed to paper No. 2, and there are no grounds to believe that this mode of "*introducing*" goods into the United States at that period was confined to Maine, or to any other part of the frontier; but on the contrary, it was familar to all, as Mr. Bradbury says, acquainted on the frontier, that the owners of the goods were the informers, when they did not intend to bring them into the United States clandestinely.

A form was adopted by the Secretary of the Treasury, after the passage of the act of February 27, which seems to have been used in all of the cases in which he remitted the fines, &c., certified by the District Judge of the District of Vermont, a copy of which, in one case, is attached to this report; and in each case the Secretary of the Treasury says, he is satisfied that the goods are *bona fide* American property; that they were not clandestinely imported or introduced since the declaration of war; and thereby the fact is most conclusively established that the goods were not seized as smuggled goods.

Distribution of fines, penalties, and forfeitures, &c.

Mr. Van Ness claims a moiety of these duties which were paid to the United States under and by virtue of an act passed on the 28th of February, 1799, 91st section, because he says he was the only custom-house officer in the District entitled to any share of the fines, &c. If he had made out a case for distribution, in my opinion, before he entitled himself to the entire moiety, he should not only show there was no other officer of the Customs, but he should show that he alone seized the goods without the aid or information of an informer; because an informer is entitled to a portion of the proceeds of the fine in cases specified in said section.

The effect of a remittance on the Collector.

Mr. Madison, in his fourth annual message to Congress on the 4th of December, 1812, stated that "a considerable number of American vessels which were in England when the revocation of the orders in council took place, were laden with British manufactures, under the erroneous impression that the non-importation act would immediately cease to operate, and would have arrived in the United States. It did not appear proper to exercise on unforseen cases of such magnitude the ordinary powers vested in the Treasury Department to mitigate forfeitures, without previously affording to Congress an opportunity of making on the subject such provisions as they may think proper. In their decision they will doubtless equally consult what is due to the equitable considerations and to the public interest."

The American merchants in nearly all of the Atlantic ports presented the same subject to Congress in their memorials. That part of the President's message which has been copied above, and the said memorials, were referred to the Committee of Ways and Means.

Among the inquires made of Mr. Gallatin, Secretary of the Treasury, was one relating to the extent of the power of the said Secretary to remit fines.

In the report of Mr. Gallatin on the 18th of November, 1812, to the inquiry mentioned he said, "of the forfeitures accrued one-half is by law vested in the custom-house officers or informers, and the other half in the United States. The power to remit the share of the United States, and of all the persons in whole or in part, and on such terms and conditions as may be deemed reasonable and just, is by law vested in the Secretary of the Treasury. But considering the magnitude and unforseen nature of the case, it was thought proper not to exercise that power or authority until Congress had taken the subject into consideration, and prescribed, if they thought proper, the course to be pursued. All the petitions already received remain therefore suspended; and in order to avoid useless expenses, the parties have been generally advised to delay making their applications in the manner directed by law until the decision of Congress could be ascertained."

Mr. Cheves, as chairman of the Committee of Ways and Means, addressed another letter to Mr. Gallatin on the 20th of November, on the subject of remission of duties, to which a reply was made on the 23d, which closed as follows:

"Upon the whole, I continue in the opinion, submitted with great deference to the Committee, that the one-half of the forfeitures which would otherwise fall to the share of the Collector, ought to be remitted; but that with respect to the other one-half belonging to the United States, justice to the community requires that, when remitted, at least an equivolent may be secured to the public for the extra profit beyond that on common importations which arises from the continuance of the non-importation act."

The merchants of Boston, New York, Philadelphia, and Baltimore, sent committees to Washington, and they were examined before the Committee of Ways and Means, touching the commercial restrictions, the interest of the American merchants, and the remission of duties. A statement was obtain from Mr Russel, then late Chargé at London.

The message, the memorials, the reports, and the depositions of the merchants, and Mr. Russel's statement, were examined and condemned by the Committee of Ways and Means, and Mr. Cheves, on the 25th of November, 1812, presented a report to the House concluding with a resolution:

"That it is inexpedient to legislate upon the subject, and that the petitions with the accompanying papers be referred to the Secretary of the Treasury."

The power was expressly asserted that the Secretary of the Treasury could remit the penalty, fine, or forfeiture, claimed by the Collector, and retain that which belonged to the United States, and that he could remit any part of either of them; and the Committee fully sanctioned the principle in the reference they proposed. Josiah Quincy, as Representative from Massachusetts, revived the same subject again at the same session of Congress, on the 20th of December, 1812, by the following resolution:

"*Resolved*, That a committee be appointed to inquire into the principles and practice adopted by the Treasury Department in relation to the revenue laws, and to the mitigating or the remitting the fines, penalties, and forfeitures accruing under the same, and that they be instructed to report thereon to the House." The resolution was adopted, and committee appointed on the 22d.

This committee corresponded with Mr. Gallatin in regard to the matters submitted to them, and he replied on the 12th of January, 1812, with great minuteness, to all the inquiries made, and stated the number of cases that had been presented for remission from 1799 to 1811, accompanied by a table showing the nett amount of fines, &c., and the expense paid during that period. The principles which governed the Secretary in remitting fines, &c., were more fully examined and explained than they had been in his communications to Mr Cheves. Mr. Quincy reported on the 27th of February, 1812, and among other things he said: "It appears to your Committee, as far as they have been enabled to judge, that the remitting and mitigating powers exercised by the Treasury Department, have been exercised in a manner liberal and just. Your committee have not deemed it their duty, from the terms of their authority, to enter into the consideration of the expediency of relieving the Treasury Department from the burden of exercising this discretion. In some commercial communities a similar discretion is invested in a board of commissioners, whose numerous members form a check upon each other, and the publicity of whose proceedings preserve their decisions under the scrutiny of the public eye, and the wholesome control of public opinion." This is the expression of another committee sanctioned by the tacit assent of the House of Representatives in favor of the power of the Secretary to remit the whole or any part of a fine, penalty, or forfeiture, without subjecting the United States to repay a collector or informer.

On the 4th of September, 1811, Samuel Buel, collector at Alburgh, in the State of Vermont, (the same district in which Mr. Van Ness was afterwards collector,) seized the sloop Hunter and 163 packages of dry goods.

The goods were appraised at $29,248 18. Information was filèd on the 4th of October in the District Court. The judge forwarded a statement of facts and petition on the 5th of October, for the remission of the fine, penalty, and forfeiture, to the Secretary of the Treasury, under the act of March 3, 1797.

Mr. Gallatin, on the 16th of November, having the application under consideration, after reciting the facts and non-importation and non-intercourse acts which had been violated, said: "I, the said Secretary of the Treasury, have maturely considered the said statements of facts and petition. Now, therefore, know ye, that I, the said Secretary of the Treasury, in consideration of the premises, and by virtue of the power and authority to me given by the said last-mentioned statute, do hereby decide to remit to the said petitioners all the right, claim, and demand of the collector only, to the forfeitures aforesaid, on payment of costs of duties, and of the remainder of the forfeitures into the Treasury, deducting from the said remainder one-half of the amount of the duties aforesaid." See Exhibit No. 3. This remission was made before the reports of the committees mentioned were presented, and the decision of Mr. Gallatin in this case was in accordance with the views which he had on both occasions expressed.

While the subject of remitting fines, forfeitures, and penalties was engaging the attention and investigation of the House of Representatives, the Senate matured a bill, which was sent to the House for concurrence on the 23d day of February, 1813; and it having been passed by that branch of Congress, it became a law on the 27th of the same month, by the approval of the President, and is the act above referred to.

The opinion of Mr. Gallatin as to the power of the Secretary of the Treasury to remit or mitigate fines, penalties, and forfeitures, is fully sustained by the Supreme Court of the United States.

Andrew Ogden, of the city of New York, in or about the month of June, 1813, imported goods into Portland, Maine, in the Brig Hollen. They were seized on the ground that they were forfeited, having been imported in violation of the non-intercourse acts, and were libelled on the 6th of July, and delivered to Andrew Ogden, the claimant, on the 19th of the same month; having been appraised and bonded, judgment of condemnation was rendered on the 27th of May, 1817; and in September of the same year judgment was entered on the bond for $22,261 75. Execution was issued, and placed in the hands of Mr. Morris, Marshal of the Southern District of New York, which he levied on certain goods, and not being sold, he was ordered by a *venditioni exponas* to offer them for sale. The Secretary of the Treasury remitted the forfeitures on conditions which the defendants complied with, and the Marshal redelivered the goods. A suit was commenced for malfeasance against Mr. Morris as Marshal, in the name of the United States, to recover the majority of the amount, for the benefit of the Collector and other officers. The question whether the Secretary of the Treasury could remit this moiety was fully presented, and the only one involved.

Mr. Wheaton and Mr. Webster were for the plaintiff, and Mr. Emmett and Mr. David B. Ogden were for the defendant. The Supreme Court of the United States gave judgment for the defendants; and Judge Thompson, in delivering the opinion of the Court, said: "We think the authority to remit is limited only to the payment of the money to the Collector for distribution. The rights and interests of these officers must necessarily be held subordinate to the authority of the United States over the subject. It is made the duty of the Collector to prosecute, and he is authorized to receive the money, and on receipt thereof, is required to distribute the same according to law. In all this, however, he acts as the agent for the Government, and subject to the authority of the Secretary of the Treasury, who may direct the prosecution to cease. And the act creating the right of the custom-house officers to a portion of the forfeitures does not vest any absolute right in them until the money is paid. To consider their right to the moiety of the forfeitures as absolute and beyond the reach of the law, after condemnation, would be subjecting the innocent to great and inequitable losses, contrary to the manifest spirit and intention of the law."

Mr. Van Ness relies on the decision of the Supreme Court in the case in error of Allen McLane *vs.* the United States.

Mr. McLane, as Collector of the District of Delaware, seized the ship Good Friends, on the 19th of April, 1812, for violating the non-intercourse laws. The libel was filed on the 5th of May; the goods were bonded and delivered to the claimants on the 9th of May, 1812; a decree of condemnation was pronounced in the District Court on the 17th of April, 1813; appealed to the Circuit Court, and affirmed on the 29th of September, 1818.

Mr. Girard, the owner, petitioned Congress to relieve him from the forfeiture in March, 1812; and on the 29th day of July, 1813, an act was passed authorizing the Secretary of the Treasury to remit the forfeiture on the payment of double duties.

On the 25th of November, 1813, Mr. McLane protested against granting any relief. The Secretary of the Treasury remitted the forfeiture on the 24th of February, 1814, on the payment of the cost and charges and duties. Congress passed an act on the 1st of July, 1812, doubling the duties.

The remission, therefore, was on the payment of double the amount, in the character of duties, of that which could have been exacted as duties at the time of the seizure. There are several discriminating features clearly distinguishing the case of Mr. McLane from that of Mr. Van Ness.

1. In the case of Mr. McLane, the forfeiture was remitted under an act of Congress passed after the interest of Mr. McLane attached, after seizure and condemnation, thereby varying the mode of dispensing relief to the claimant; whereas in the case of Mr. Van Ness there was no changes in the law or mode of relief.

2. This claim is made under and in consequence of the decision in the case of Mr. McLane. That case was argued by the counsel of Mr. McLane, and decided by the Court, on the ground, inchoate right of the Collector on the seizure of the goods was so far vested and perfect right, that it could not be divested or prejudiced by any subsequent act of Congress, passed after the seizure of the goods.

Mr. McLane protested against the remission at the time, and never acquiesced in it for a moment; while Mr. Van Ness acquiesced in the remission of the forfeitures at and for more than thirty years afterwards, rendered and settled his accounts accordingly, took bonds for the duties secured and restored to the Government in pursuance of the decisions of the Secretary of the Treasury, in remitting the forfeiture collected, and paid the amount into the Treasury, after deducting the ordinary commission allowed to him on all duties collected.

3. In the case of Mr. McLane double duties were levied after the ship Good Friends and cargo were seized. In the case of Mr. Van Ness there was no increase of duties between the time of seizure and that of remission.

The Court say, "The question then arises, in what light the reservation and payment of the double duties as conditions upon which the remission is granted are to be considered? Are the double duties to be deemed a mere payment of lawful duties, or are they to be deemed a part of the cargo? If the latter be the true construction, then the collector is entitled to a moiety; if the former, he is barred of all claim."

The Court decided that under the circumstances of that, the double duties which were reserved were a forfeiture, and therefore that Mr. McLane was entitled to a moiety.

The decision in the case of the United States *vs.* Morris, was not overruled, but the facts in the case of McLane so far varied from that of Morris, as to require a different decision as to the law.

The Comptroller is requested to state "the amount that will probably be required to provide for all claims which may be established upon the principles set forth in the petition of Mr. Van Ness."

This amount cannot be ascertained with certainty. From information derived from those formerly in this office, and acquainted with accounts of Collectors of Customs, I believe that the money that was paid by the importers under remission of fines, penalties, and forfeitures, by the Secretary of the Treasury, is placed under the head of "duties on merchandise."

Mr. Gallatin, in his letter of the 18th of November, 1812, referred to above, estimated the bonds which had been executed for goods imported in contravention of law, after the 23d of June, 1812, would fall some short of $18,000,000, exclusively of the bonds given for duties, which he said might be estimated at $5,000,000.

He thought this sum would not be materially increased by vessels still on their way, unless it should be true, as had been stated, that American vessels which had sailed to the Baltic under certain British licenses, should, on their arrival in England, be provided with new licenses for their return to the United States with cargoes of British merchandise.

The amount of duties collected in 1813, was - - -	$7,200,583 28
" " " " 1814, " - - -	4,241,482 06

How much of this sum was paid in the character of duties after the goods were seized *pro forma*, as mentioned above, I cannot ascertain, but the petitioner bases his claim on the asserted fact, that all importations in 1813 and 1814 were unlawful, and that no legal duties could have been collected, "as the importation," "or introduction," was in violation of the non-importation acts of Congress then in force. If the complainant is entitled to a moiety of the duties so received by him, I do not know why all other collectors and their officers may not be entitled to a moiety of the duties collected as the duties were in Passamquoddy, Maine, as stated by Trescott, the collector, and cited above—

The amount estimated by Mr. Gallatin for duties in 1812, to November 18, is - - - - - -	$5,000,000 00
The amount shown by the public accounts in 1813 and 1814, is - - - - - - - - - -	11,442,065 34
	$16,442,065 34

It appears from the public accounts, that the amount of duties collected at Alburgh, Vermont, in 1812, by Mr. Buel and Mr. Van Ness, was $95,330 93. He says about $34,000 were paid in the Treasury as duties, when the goods were seized, and fines, &c. were remitted on pay in the duties. If the same proportion of the $16,442,065 34 arose from the payment of the duties where the fines, &c. were remitted, the amount derived, this was $5,864,101 20; a moiety of which is $2,932,050 60, which might be demanded at the Treasury if Congress should think proper to grant relief to Mr. Van Ness.

In conclusion, I report distinctly on the different points, as directed by the Secretary of the Treasury.

1st. "Showing what evidence remains in the files of this department not only in regard to this claim, but other similar cases."

Report.—There is no original evidence in regard to this or similar claims, except the books containing "general accounts of the receipts and expenditures of the United States for each year, stated in pursuance of the standing order of the House of Representatives of the United States, passed on the 30th day of December, one thousand seven hundred and ninety-one," and the public documents which are printed.

2d. The action of the Government in similar cases.

Report.—In all cases of seizure of a similar character to the case of Mr. Van Ness, the practice has been to make application to the Secretary of the Treasury, by petition, accompanied by a statement of facts made by a judge of a court of the United States; and, on a hearing, the Secretary of the Treasury has relinquished such part of the fine, penalty, and forfeiture as he thought proper, or the whole of it, or the whole of the moiety claimed by the informer, if such remission is before the goods, &c. have been sold and the money made, and until the money has been made and ready for distribution, the right of the informer has been considered inchoate; but after the money has been made and ready for distribution, then it has been considered that the informer's right is vested and beyond the power of the Secretary of the Treasury to relinquish.

3d. The amount that will probably be required to provide for all claims which may be established upon the principles set forth in the petition of Mr. Van Ness.

Report.—Not far from three millions of dollars.

4. To furnish such explanations and observations as shall enable Congress to act with full knowledge of the consequences.

Report.—The explanations are made above by referring to the laws and documents applicable to the case.

Most respectfully submitted,

ELISHA WHITTLESEY.

Hon. W. M. Meredith,
Secretary of the Treasury.

Exhibit No. 1—referred to on page 11.
Mr. Bradbury's paper, No. 2.

The following are the several parcels of plaster paris, salt, and grindstones, which have been seized in the District of Passamaquoddy since the declaration of war and before the 26th of February, 1813, of which petitions have been presented to the Judge of the District Court of Maine for a remission of the forfeitures, viz:

Seward Buckram	128	tons	plaster	paris.
Isaac Lukeman	300	do	do	do
Jabez Moury	123	do	do	do
do	470	do	do	do
do	200	do	do	do
Samuel Wheeler and others	250	do	do	do
Jabez Moury	800	grindstones.		
do	1,426	do		
Sumuel Wheeler and others	1,800	bushels salt.		
Robert Dutch	1,000	do		

The above plaster paris, salt, and grindstones, have been seized in this District on information of the several claimants since the declaration of war, and before the 26th day of February, 1813, information having been previously given me by the several claimants of their intention to bring into the United States the within mentioned plaster paris, salt, and grindstones, and deliver the same into my hands, and it does not appear that the claimants intended to avoid a scrutiny of the custom-house officers.

L. TRESCOTT,
Collector.

April 13, 1813.

EXHIBIT No. 1—REFERRED TO ON PAGE 11.

Mr. Bradbury's paper, No. 3.

The following is a statement of the several parcels of British manufactured goods which have been seized in the District of Passamquoddy since the declaration of war, and before the 26th day of February, 1813, and for which petitions to the Judge of the District Court have been presented for a remission of forfeitures, viz:

No.	Claimant	Property
No. 1.	Caleb Starks and Henry Smith,	Schr. Cranbury and cargo.
2.	Samuel Denton, - - - - -	Rising Sun and cargo.
3.	Lewis Tappan, George Searl, and B. L. Swan, - - - -	Nymph and cargo.
4.	Robert Cummings, - - -	Twenty-seven puncheons rum. Twelve puncheons rum. Forty-two barrels sugar. Eleven barrels sugar.
5.	Samuel and John Buck, - - -	Ten hogsheads rum.
6.	Jonathan Bartlett and others,	159 Packages glass and hardware goods shipped to Portland in the Raven and Lively.
7.	Samuel Torry, - - - - - -	78 hogsheads merchandise.
8.	Seward Buckram, - - - - -	55 casks and 5 packages goods.
9.	Charles Tappan - - - - -	25 and 33 packages goods.
10.	Seward Buckram, - - - - -	50 crates earthenware.
11.	Sam'l Archer, Stanly B. Bishopman, Josiah Longstreth, and Edward Weston -	8 casks merchandise.
12.	Charles N. Banker - - - -	1 gundola and 74 bales goods.
13.	Joseph Woodwards, jr. - - -	724 packages goods.
14.	William Long - - - - -	40 trunks and 23 bales merchandise, a part of the cargo of sloop Henry.
15.	Nathan Buckram - - - -	27 packages and 11 casks glass ware and 3 boxes containing 51 pieces cloth.
16.	Hugh K. Toter - - - -	Sch'r Polly and cargo, consisting of 13 cases, 14 trunks and 15 bales British manufactured goods.
17.	Cha's. Bind and others - - -	Sloop Henry and others.
18.	Francis Boot - - - - - - -	Sloop Henry.
19.	Jabez Mouny - - - - - - -	12 Puncheons rum.

Previous to the above and the within mentioned merchandise being delivered to me, the claimants had called on me at the custom-house and informed me of their intention to bring the above and within mentioned merchandise into the United States, and to deliver the same to me as Collector of the district of Passamaquoddy, and there did not appear (as far as came to my knowledge) the least appearance of a clandestine introduction of the before mentioned goods into the United States.

August 13, 1813. L. TRESCOTT,
Collector.

Exhibit No. 2.—referred to on page 12.

To all to whom these presents shall come: I, Alexander James Dallas, *Secretary of the Treasury of the United States, send greeting:*

Whereas, a statement of facts bearing date the 2d of September, 1814, with the petition of David Stone, of Walpole, N. H., thereto annexed, touches the forfeitures and penalties which by reason of the importation of certain merchandise from Canada, having been incurred under the statute of the United States, entitled "An act to interdict the commercial intercourse between the United States and Great Britain and France and their dependencies, and for other purposes;" and a statute supplementary to the last mentioned statute, has been transmitted to the Secretary of the Treasury by the Judge of the United States for the district of Vermont, in pursuance to the statute of the United States entitled "An act directing the Secretary of the Treasury to remit certain fines, penalties, and forfeitures therein mentioned," as by the said statement of facts and petition remaining in the Treasury Department of the United States may fully appear: And, whereas, I, the said Secretary of the Treasury, have maturely considered the said statement of facts and petition: and whereas, it has been proved to my satisfaction, that the goods, wares, and merchandise, by the importation whereof the forfeitures and penalties aforesaid have been incurred, were, at the time of the importation into the United States, *bona fide* American property, that they were not clandestinely imported, and that they were imported since the declaration of war;

Now, therefore, know ye, That I, the said Secretary of the Treasury, in consideration of the premises, and by virtue of the power and authority to me given by the said last mentioned statute, do hereby decide to remit the petitioner aforesaid all the fines, penalties, and forfeitures, incurred as aforesaid, upon the cost and charges that have arisen, or may arise, being paid, and upon payment of the duties which would have been payable on the goods, wares, and merchandise, if legally imported; and also do hereby direct the prosecution, or prosecutions, if any shall have been instituted, for the recovery thereof, to cease and to be discontinued on payment of the costs, charges, and duties, as aforesaid.

Given under my hand and seal of office, in the city of Washington, this twelfth day of May, in the year of our Lord one thousand eight hundred and fifteen, and thirty-ninth year of the Independence of the United States.

A. J. DALLAS,
Secretary of the Treasury

Exhibit No. 3—referred to on page 15.

To all whom these presents shall come, I, Albert Gallatin, Secretary of the Treasury of the United States, send greeting:

Whereas, as a statement of facts bearing date the 5th day of October, 1811, with the petition of Matthias Bruen and Frederick Sheldon, of New York, merchants, thereto annexed, touching certain forfeitures incurred under the statute of the United States, entitled "An act to interdict the commercial intercourse between the United States and Great Britain and France, and their dependencies, and for other purposes," has been submitted to the Secretary of the Treasury of the United States, by the Judge of the United States for the District of Vermont, pursuant to the statute of the United States, entitled "An act to provide for mitigating or remitting the forfeitures, fines and penalties, and disabilities occcurring on certain cases therein mentioned," as by the said statement of facts and petition remaining in the Treasury Department of the United States, may fully appear: And whereas, I, the said Secretary of the Treasury, have maturely considered the said statement of facts and petition;

Now, therefore, know ye, That I, the said Secretary of the Treasury, in consideration of the premises, and by virtue of the power and authority to me given by the said last-mentioned statute, do hereby remit to the said petitioner all the right, claim, and demand of the Collector only, to the forfeitures aforesaid, on the payment of costs of duties, and of the remainder of the forfeitures into the Treasury, deducting from the said remainder one-half of the amount of the duties aforesaid.

Given under my hand and seal of office, in the city of Washington, this sixteenth day of November, in the year of our Lord one thousand eight hundred and twelve, and the 37th of the Independence of the United States.

ALBERT GALLATIN,
Secretary of the Treasury.

Exhibit No. 4.—(*Copy.*)

Entry of nine hogsheads, two bales, and nine trunks of merchandise imported from the Province of Lower Canada into the district of Vermont, by Ithamar Eaton, of Burlington, Vermont, agent for Arthur Tappan, and seized and libelled on behalf of the United States, and restored on bonds agreeably to law to wait the event of the prosecution.

Marks.	Number.	Packages and contents.	Virtue subject to 27½ ad valorem.
E	5, 3, 41, 9, 7, 12, 126, 8	Nine hhds. cloths, kerseymeres and vestings.	£855 5 5
A	18, 9, 3	One bale, Two trunks } Blankets. - - - -	14 15 0
7 trunks, and 1 bale furniture			£870 0 5

Burlington, April 28, 1813. ITHAMAR EATON.

Duties on this entry, 27½ ad valorem, $1,168 51.

C. P. VAN NESS, *Collector.*

District of Vermont, *Port of Alburgh.*

I, Ithamar Eaton, do solemnly, sincerely, and truely swear, that the entry now subscribed with my name, and delivered by me to the Collector for the District of Vermont, contains a just and true account of all the goods, wares, and merchandise seized and prosecuted as is set forth in said entry, and that the said entry contains a just and true account in sterling money of the cost of said goods, that the invoice now produced by me is the true, genuine, and only invoice by me received of the said goods, wares, and merchandise contained in the said entry, and the only by which I have been charged, and for which I am to account, and that the said invoice in the actual state in which received by me, and that I do not know of any other invoice or account of the said goods, wares, and merchandise different from what is here produced. I do further swear that if I hereafter discover any other or greater quantity of goods, wares, and merchandise than is contained in the entry aforesaid, or shall receive of the whole or any part thereof, other in quantity, quality, and than have now been exhibited, I will and without delay report the same to the Collector of this district. I also swear that nothing has been concealed or suppressed in the said entry, whereby to avoid the just payment of the duties imposed by the laws of the United States, and that all matters are justly and truely expressed therein according to my best knowledge and belief. So help me God. ITHAMAR EATON.

Exhibit No. 5.

A list of papers relating to the case of C. P. Van Ness.

The following, received from the office of the Commissioner of Customs, being copies of papers procured by Mr. Feran, a clerk, who was sent under instructions from the Department to obtain information from the different custom houses in relation to this class of cases.

Statement of actions that were instituted under the non-importation and non-intercourse laws of the U. S. for the years of 1809–'10–'11–'12 '13 and '14 for the District of Boston and Charlestown.

Abstracts, 69 in number, of cases in Rem, and copies of remissions belonging to the same cases, furnished by E. H. Prentiss, a clerk, Montpelier, Vt.

List of seizures at Portland from 1808 to 1818.

Letter from Bion Bradbury, collector of Passamaquoddy, in relation to revenue cases during the war of 1812, and the period immediately preceding, with six documents accompaying the same.

Abstracts of suits brought by the United States in the Eastern District of Pennsylvania, for the breach of non-intercourse laws.

Report of facts relating to goods imported in the District of Delaware, in violation of the non-intercourse laws, during the years 1809–'10–'11 and '12, with accompanying documents four in number.

Petition of John Noble of London, by his attorney, Thomas N. Lee, of Petersburg, Va., for a remission of forfeiture under the non-intercourse laws of 1809 and 1810.

The above papers have been returned to the files of the office of the Commissioner of Customs.

22 papers endorsed "Abstract of Interest."
22 " " "Accounts of Liquidated Bonds" and
"Accounts current of Liquidated Bonds."
21 " " "Accounts Current," and
"General Account Current."
1 " " "Bond Account Current."
1 " " "Bond Account."
1 " " "Custom House Bonds delivered James Fisk."
2 corrected Treasury Statements.
1 " "Account of Costs."
1 copy of Mr. Van Ness's letter to Comptroller, Nov. 1, 1816.
4 Letters from Comptroller to Mr. Van Ness.
1 Petition of C. P. Van Ness.

It is believed that the above described papers were left in this office by Mr. Van Ness. They appear to be copies from the files and records of the custom-house in the district of Vermont.

WASHINGTON, *April* 29, 1852.

To the Hon. A. P. BUTLER, *Chairman of the Committee on the Judiciary of the Senate of the U. S.*

SIR: About five years ago I addressed to the Congress of the United States a petition setting forth a claim which I believed, and still believe, to be just and legal, in my favor, upon the Government of the United States. That petition having been presented to the Senate and referred to the Committee on the Judiciary in that body, it was transmitted by that committee to the Secretary of the Treasury, with the request that he would furnish such information as his Department might possess in regard to the said claim, and the Secretary sent the same to the First Comptroller for his report thereon.

A report was accordingly made by Comptroller McCulloh, in which it is stated that, on due examination, it was ascertained that I had paid into the Treasury of the United States, in the manner alleged in my petition, the sum of $36,353, and that a moiety of the said sum at the time of such payment lawfully belonged to me. The Secretary, however, on receiving that report, sent the same back to the Comptroller for *further* information, which, it was supposed, the committee was desirious to obtain.

A change afterwards took place in the office of Comptroller, and Mr. McCulloh, before making any further report, was succeeded by Mr. Whittlesey. This latter officer has made another report, in which, besides furnishing the additional information which he professed to consider as embraced by the letter of the Secretary, he has gone into a long and elaborate course of remarks in opposition to my claim, and to the opinion of Mr. McCulloh. The two reports, I understand, are now before your committee. The first was made by an able and distinguished lawyer and public officer; and the last by one whose measure of ability, in either capacity, will be developed as we proceed in this investigation. In my reply to that of Mr. Whittlesey, I shall be compelled to enter a good deal into detail on account of the enormous mass of irrelevant and immaterial matter of which he has delivered himself; but I feel quite confident that it will not be a difficult task to show that the offspring of his labors has neither law nor fact to sustain it.

He sets out by saying, "The commencement of Mr. Van Ness's term as collector in Vermont was on the 15th of February, 1813, as stated by him, but its termination is a subject of some doubt." And afterwards he says, "It is supposed that the original accounts and vouchers of Mr. Van Ness, as collector, were destroyed by the fire which consumed the Treasury building."

Now, will it not appear surprising to the committee to be informed that every original account, and every voucher, which I rendered to the Treasury during the five years of my collectorship in Vermont, ever has been, and now is, to be found in the Treasury Department, with the single exception of the detailed quarterly bond accounts. And of these bond accounts I have produced complete duplicates, with the affidavit on each one proving its accuracy, by the person who, as my clerk at the time, made out both the originals forwarded to the Treasury and the duplicates retained by me. And besides this, these duplicates are verified by the general quarterly accounts in the Treasury, since, at the end of each quarter, the balance of bonds on hand is brought into the general account, and this, in every instance, agrees precisely with the balance in my duplicate bond account of the corresponding quarter. Moreover, this is fully explained by the report of Mr. McCulloh, which Mr. Whittlesey had in his possession when he made his own.

As to the termination of my collectorship, there is no more difficulty in ascertaining its date, than there is that of its commencement. My accounts in the Treasury came up to the first day of February, 1818; and in the last one are charged the bonds and other property delivered over to my successor, J. Fisk, Esq. And the accounts of Mr. Fisk, commencing on that day, are likewise in the Treasury.

I beg leave here to notice a fact of a singular character, though in itself, or as relating to this case, of no importance. In connexion with quite a long story about the difficulty of finding out when my term of office expired, Mr. Whittlesey states, that in March, 1816, I was appointed a commissioner on the boundary line under the treaty of Ghent, and that I settled my accounts as such commissioner in the year 1823, giving at the same time the items of that account.

Now, if the learned Comptroller really entertained so low an opinion of the members of Congress, as to suppose that in their examination and decision of the claim which I have presented, they would be influenced by the consideration that I had held the office of a boundary commissioner and received the salary attached to it, he might surely have introduced that matter without doing it at the expense of acknowledging his ignorance of a fact (the time of my leaving the collectorship) of which any clerk in his office could have informed him. And let it be understood, too, that he has suggested no incompatibility in my holding the two offices at the same time, nor any question of my having fully accounted for all moneys received by me. And lastly, it will be seen that the seizures of the goods from which the money claimed by me has arisen, took place during the years 1813 and 1814, so that had I left office at the end of those two years, my rights would have been precisely the same as they are now.

The seizures in question all took place under the non-intercourse acts, which prohibited, under the penalty of forfeiture, the importation of any merchandise from the Kingdom of Great Britain, or from any colony or dependency thereof. And all moneys arising from such seizures were to be distributed—the one moiety to the United States, and the other moiety to the collectors, naval officers, and surveyors, or to such of the said officers as there might be, at the time, in the districts where the seizures were made. In Vermont there was only a collector, and of course he was entitled to an entire moiety of the proceeds of all seizures made during his time.

But the learned Comptroller says that even if I should make out a case for distribution, before I could entitle myself to a moiety of the money in question, I ought not only to show that there was no naval officer or surveyor in my district, but also that I seized the goods without the aid of an informer, who might be entitled to a share of the collector's moiety.

The proper mode of ascertaining whether there was any naval officer or surveyor in the Vermont district is, by the records and accounts in the Comptroller's own office; and those will show that there never has been, to the present time, any other officer than the collector in that district.

As to there having been *informers* or not, in my cases, it might be sufficient for me to say that I could not be called upon to prove a negative of that sort, even if the cases had been such as to admit of informers, which they were not. The importations, although against law, and incurring forfeitures, were open and public, and not actually of a *fraudulent* or *smuggling* character. And the idea which has been suggested in some part of the report, to which I am replying, that the owners or importers of the goods could be considered as informers, because they may have given previous notice of their intention to bring in the goods, has no foundation in reason or law.

The acts passed during that period authorizing or directing remissions, were made applicable only to cases where the importations were *not clandestine;* and hence the object and necessity on the part of the importers of giving previous notice of their intentions to the officers of Government, but they could not thereby acquire an interest in that portion of the forfeiture which was reserved as a substitute for duties, and which they offered and expected to pay, and to the retention of which by the Government they assented, by the acceptance of the terms and conditions of the remissions. Moreover, the contrary position would lead to the singular result, that the importers in such cases would, in reality, pay only three-fourths of the amount for which they would be liable on a legal importation.

An *informer*, within the meaning of the law, is one through whose information an attempted or intended *fraud* upon the Government is detected. And if we suppose a case of actual *smuggling*, it is hardly to be believed that the smuggler would inform against himself, or if he did, that he could acquire the right to pocket a portion of the forfeiture incurred by his own deliberate and wilful violation of the laws.

By the act of March 3d, 1797, the Secretary of the Treasury has the power to remit all penalties and forfeitures in cases where there has been no wilful negligence nor intention of fraud. And the non-intercourse acts authorized remissions of forfeitures under them in the same manner.

Soon after the declaration of war against England in 1812, considerable quantities of merchandise arrived in our ports from England, having been shipped previous to a knowledge of the war. Other quantities had been sent to Canada to wait the course of events there. All these goods were seized and libelled as forfeited under the non-intercourse laws. But the owners applied for remissions of the forfeitures.

Mr. Gallatin, who was then Secretary of the Treasury, considered that he had the power, under the existing law, to remit the forfeitures; but as the amount was large, he deemed it proper to submit the subject to the action of Congress. The result was that two acts were passed for the relief of the importers—the one on the 2d January, 1813, in relation to the importations direct from the Kingdom of Great Britain; and the other on the 27th of February of the same year, concerning importations from the British dependencies. These acts *directed* the Secretary of the Treasury to make remissions on proof of certain facts; but they did not interfere with the *discretionary* power conferred on him by the act of 1797.

The learned Comptroller says, in speaking of the act of February 27th, 1813, "The Secretary of the Treasury and the courts of the United States construed this act prospectively, as well as to the transactions before its date, and the duties remitted during the time Mr. Van Ness was in office were by virtue of its provisions, so far as the northern frontier was concerned." All that is correct of this statement is, that the Secretary appears in one case to have made a remission under the act in the case of a seizure made after its passage, but he was soon stopped by the courts. In the case of the Margaretta and her cargo, reported in the 2d vol. of Gallison, the very question arose whether the Secretary had the power by this act to remit a forfeiture incurred after its passage, and Judge Story disposed of it in the following terms: "The importation in the present case is conceded on all sides to have been made in September, 1813, at least six months after the passage of the act. If, therefore, it be not prospective in its operations, it is very clear that the remission is utterly void. It seems to me that upon no reasonable construction, consistent with the apparent intention or the language of the statute, can it be deemed to apply to future cases."

Congress gave the same construction to the act that Judge Story did, and previous to the decision of that Judge, passed an act on the 28th July, 1813, placing certain importations from Canada, by Thomas Denny, after the date of the act, upon the same ground as if they had taken place before its passage. And on the 12th February, 1814, an act was passed placing certain importations by William Slothart and Josiah Starkey, after the passage of the act of the 2d January, 1813, upon the same ground as if made before the date of that act.

Nor is it a fact that all the remissions in my cases were by virtue of the act of February, 1813. Several of them were in cases which had occurred after the date of that act, and were made under the general and discretionary power conferred upon the Secretary by the law of 1797.

It is true that Mr. Gallatin was of opinion that he could remit the collector's share of a forfeiture, and retain that of the United States; and he had exercised that power in one or two instances anterior to the period in question. But it is not true, as stated by the learned Comptroller, that this opinion was sustained by the Supreme Court, in the case of the United States against Morris, marshal of New York. The question in that case was not whether the Secretary could remit the share of the collector and retain that of the United States, but whether the share of the collector could be remitted at all after judgment of condemnation. There was a remission of the whole forfeiture, with a reservation of a small portion, not for the United States, but for the collector. The court decided that the power of remission continued to the time of the receipt of the money by the collector for distribution.

On the contrary, it has been fully settled by the courts that the Secretary could *not* remit the share of the collector, and reserve that of the United States. In the case already referred to of the Margaretta, Judge Story declared that the Secretary "could not remit the collector's share *eo nomine;*" and in the case of the executor of Allen McLane against the United States, reported in the 6th vol. of Peters's Reports, page 404, and to which I shall have occasion more at large to refer, the Supreme Court says: "The Government has no authority under the existing laws to release the collector's share, as such, and yet to retain to itself the other part of the forfeiture."

The acts of January 2d and of February 27th, 1813, directed the remission to be made upon the condition or reservation of payment of the duties that would have been payable by law on such goods, wares, and merchandise, if legally imported, and of all costs and charges of prosecution. And all the remissions in my cases, whether made under those acts or under the old law of 1797, were precisely upon these terms and conditions. And the sums thus reserved were directed by the Government to be paid into the Treasury, and the amount so paid by me was $36,353.

I will now proceed to show that a moiety of this money lawfully belonged to me at the time it went into the Treasury; that question having been directly and fully settled by the Supreme Court of the United States in the case already referred to of McLane against the U. States.

It appears that Allen McLane, as Collector of the District of Delaware, in April, 1812, seized the ship Good Friends and her cargo for a violation of the same non-intercourse acts under which all my seizures were made. The ship and cargo were libelled before the proper court, and were condemned in April, 1813. An appeal was taken to a higher court, and while that appeal was pending in July, 1813, an act was passed by Congress extending to the case the benefits of the act of the 2d January, 1813. In January, 1814, there was a remission by the Secretary of the Treasury in the same terms and upon the same conditions as in my cases. Upon these facts the case came before the Supreme Court.

It appears further that Collector McLane, in the first place, had objected to the remission upon the ground that his right, as the seizing officer, could not be divested after the condemnation by the district court. But that objection was abandoned, and the case was brought before the Supreme Court, and argued and decided, simply upon the question whether the collector was entitled or not to *a moiety of the sum reserved in the remission*, which was as in my cases the amount which the duties would have been on a legal importation. Consequently the decision in that case equally settles the law in mine.

But here it becomes necessary to make some further exposures of the errors of understanding of Comptroller Whittlesey. In the first place, he appears to be confused with regard to the question of double duties, which, though introduced into the case of McLane, had no connexion with the real point in dispute. The goods in that case had been imported and seized previous to the act of July, 1812, imposing the double duties, but, in making the remission, the Secretary thought it proper to reserve the amount of the double duties. It was, however, admitted at the Treasury that the increased amount thus reserved might be considered as *forfeiture*, and the moiety of it paid to the collector. This appears in the case and was admitted before the court, so that the only question was, whether the single duties, or rather the existing duties on legal importations, at the time of that importation and seizure, should be considered as duties exacted, or as a reservation of so much of the forfeiture, and of which the collector was entitled to a moiety.

In my case the seizures were all after the act imposing the additional or double duties, and consequently the reservation of the amount equal to these duties is of the same character, and to be governed by the same principles, as the single duties in the McLane case. The court proceeded upon tho ground that there *could* be no duties on prohibited goods, and that whatever was reserved, no matter under what name, was so much of the forfeiture, and to be divided between the Government and the collector.

The learned Comptroller then proceeds to say that "there are several discriminating features distinguishing the case of McLane from that of Mr. Van Ness;" and the first one he points out is, that "in the case of McLane the forfeiture was remitted under an act of Congress passed after his interest had attached by seizure and condemnation, thereby varying the mode of dispensing relief to the claimant; whereas, in the case of Van Ness there were no changes in the law or mode of relief;" and soon afterwards he declares that the case of McLane "was argued by counsel, and decided by the court, on the ground that the inchoate right of the collector was so far a vested and perfect right, that it could not be divested or prejudiced by any subsequent act of Congress passed after the seizure of the goods." Now all this is wholly without foundation, both as to fact and law.

So far from there having been no changes in the laws, after the seizures in my cases, it is a fact that in the greater portion of them the remissions were made under laws passed after the seizures had taken place, and we have already seen that the acts of January 2d and February 27th, 1813, were passed only for seizures already made, and *could not* apply to future cases. We have also seen that the Comptroller himself has spoken of the act last mentioned as "applicable to transactions before its date," and as *legalizing* the importations to which it applied. And now, after all this, he turns round and asserts that it was decided in the McLane case that the collector's right could not be divested or prejudiced by an act passed after the seizure.

Is it not wonderful that it did not occur to the acute and discriminating mind of the learned Comptroller, that if the case of McLane had been argued and decided upon the ground stated by him, the collector in that case would have been entitled to a moiety of the whole appraised value of the ship and cargo? Why, the right of the Government to remit the whole or any portion of the forfeiture, under the act passed for that purpose after the seizure, was not even called in question. The only point in dispute, as has been already stated, was whether the collector was divested of his right to share with the Government whatever was *not* remitted, but reserved in lieu of duties. And it was precisely *this* right which the court said he could not be divested of by an act passed after the seizure.

The Comptroller further says, that Collector McLane protested against the remission in his case, while I acquiesced in those in my cases. Well, what if this should be so? Mr. McLane's protest was of no benefit to him, so far as it regarded the amount that was remitted; and my acquiesence as to the portions remitted in my cases could have no effect upon my right to share with the Government the portions that were not remitted.

But I will here introduce the material part of the decision of the Supreme Court in the McLane case, by which it will be seen how fully and clearly the principles upon which my claim is founded were sustained and settled.

"The question then arises, in what light the reservation and payment of the double duties, as conditions upon which the remission is granted, are to be considered? Are the double duties to be deemed a mere payment of lawful duties; or are they to be deemed a part of the forfeiture reserved out of the proceeds of the cargo? If the latter be the true construction, then the collector is entitled to a moiety; if the former, he is barred of all claim.

"The duty of the Collector in superintending the collection of the revenue, and making seizures for supposed violations of law, is onerous, and full of perplexity. If he seizes any goods, it is at his own peril; and he is condemnable in damages and costs, if it shall turn out, upon the final adjudication, that there was no probable cause for the seizure. As a just reward for his diligence, and a compensation for his risks, at once to stimulate his vigilance, and to secure his activity, the laws of the United States have awarded to him a large share of the proceeds of the forfeiture. But his right by the seizure, is but in cohate, and although the forfeiture may have been justly incurred, yet the Government has reserved to itself the right to release it, either in whole or in part, until the proceeds have been actually received for distribution; and, in that event, and to that extent, it displaces the right of the collector. Such was the decision of this Court in the case of the United States against Morris, 10 Wheaton's Reports, 246. But whatever is reserved by the Government out of the forfeiture, is reserved as well for the seizing officer as for itself, and is distributable accordingly. The Government has no authority under the existing laws to release the Collector's share as such, and yet to retain to itself the other part of the forfeiture.

"In the present case it is perfectly clear that the seizure of the Good Friends and her cargo was justifiable, that they were forfeited for a violation of the non-intercourse acts. This is established not only by the final decree of condemnation, but by the very terms of the remission granted by the Secretary of the Treasury. In point of law, no duties, as such, can legally accrue upon the importation of prohibited goods. They are not entitled to entry at the custom-house, or to be bonded.

"They are, *ipso facto*, forfeited by the mere act of importation. The Good Friends, then, having arrived in April, 1812, long before the double duties were laid, and her cargo being prohibited from importation, it is impossible, in a legal sense, to sustain the argument, that the importation could be deemed innocent, and the Government could be entitled to duties as upon a lawful importation. It was entitled to the whole property, by way of forfeiture, and to nothing by way of duties. When, therefore, Congress authorized the remission upon the payment of double duties, the latter was imposed as a condition of restitution upon the offending party. In the language of the act of the 2d January, 1813, the remission was to be "on payment of the duties which would have been payable by law on such goods, wares, and merchandise, if legally imported;" not upon payment of the duties which had lawfully accrued upon the same goods. The act presupposes that no duties had accrued, or could accrue, by operation of law upon the goods; and the act of the 26th of July, 1813, expressly treats it as a condition. Indeed, it is impossible it could lawfully have accrued upon the importation of the cargo of the Good Friends in April, 1812, when the double duties were not imposed until the passage of the act of the 1st of July of the same year.

"If the Government had reserved a gross sum equivalent to the double duties, as a condition of the remission, there could be no doubt that the Collector would have been entitled to his moiety of the sum so reserved. Can it make any difference in point of law, that the reservation is made by a reference to double duties, as a mode of ascertaining that sum? It has not been pretended that the act of the 29th of July, 1813, could divest the rights of the Collector, antecedently vested in him by the existing laws. And if such a doctrine could be maintained at all, it would still be necessary to establish that there was an unequivocal intention on the part of the Government to remit his share, and to retain its own share of the forfeiture. Such an extraordinary exercise of power, if it could be even maintained, where it is subversive of existing rights, ought to be evidenced by terms susceptible of no doubt. We are of opinion that the present act neither justifies nor requires any such construction. The double duties are referred to as a mere mode of ascertaining the amount intended to be reserved out of the forfeiture, and not as a declaration of intention on the part of the Government that they were to be received as legal duties due upon a legal importation.

"But a distinction has been taken at the argument on behalf of the United States, and an apportionment or division of the duties has been insisted on. It is said that so much of the duties demanded as were equal to the single duties payable by law on imported goods in April, 1812, ought to be considered as received in that character by the Government, since this case has been treated by the Government as an innocent importation. But as to the additional duties imposed by the act of the 1st of July, 1812, they may be considered as a reservation of forfeiture. And it is added that the Government has itself acted upon this distinction in this very case; for it has allowed the Collector his moiety of the latter, and denied it in respect to the former.

"The true answer to be given to this argument is, that the act itself contemplates no such apportionment or division of the duties, the duties are reserved as a whole, and not in moieties, and it could not well be otherwise, for as has been already shown, no duties at all were legally payable on the goods. They were in fact, and were treated by the Government as prohibited goods. And when the Government imposed the double duties as a condition, they were imposed as a sum which would have accrued upon a legal importation after the 1st of July, 1812. The very circumstance that the Government itself has treated any part of the reservation as forfeiture and as distributable accordingly, is conclusive to show that the whole is incapable of being treated as duties. The distinction contended for, then, not being found in the act itself, and part of it being confessedly received in the character of a forfeiture, we think the whole must be treated as received as a reservation by way of forfeiture. Our opinion is grounded upon the fact, that the act refers to the double duties as a mere mode of ascertaining the amount; and that it is undistinguishable from the case of a reservation of a gross sum."

And now let me ask, if I have succeeded in showing that the money in question was mine at the time it went into the Treasury, and was paid over in obedience to the directions of my superiors in office, and in ignorance of my rights, what good reason can exist why it should not be returned to me? It is true there has been a delay in the presentation of my claim, but that is fully explained in my petition, and it has been shown that all the facts of the case have been as clearly proved as they could have been one year after the claim accrued.

It appears that in the case of Collector McLane—who had not the same reasons for delay which I have shown—the money had been paid to the Government nearly twenty years before his claim was brought before the Court; yet, as soon the decision was made, the amount of his claim was allowed to him at the Treasury without any act of Congress. My rights are precisely the same as his were, and why should a return of my money be refused?

I appeal, therefore, to the justice and equity of Congress. I could have legally retained this money out of funds of the Government which have since passed through my hands, but I would not adopt a course of that kind. What I claim I seek to obtain by the voluntary action of the Government.

Comptroller Whittlesey has expressed the opinion that there were paid into the Treasury about $3,000,000 in the same way as the money claimed by me. Well, if there is really so much money in the Treasury belonging to individuals, why should it be withheld from them? Surely the *right* cannot be dependent upon the *amount.* But it may be considered very doubtful whether claims to the amount of a thirtieth, or even a sixtieth, part of the sum estimated by him, will ever be established, even if claimed.

A single glance at the manner in which Mr. Whittlesey has arrived at his conclusion upon this point, will be sufficient to confirm what I have said. He informs us that the amount of duties collected at the Treasury in the year 1813, was $7,200,583 28; and in the year 1814, $4,241,482 06—making for the two years $11,442,065 34; then he adds to this amount the sum of $5,000,000 which Mr. Gallatin, in November, 1812, estimated as the *probable* amount of duties on the merchandise then under seizure, and on account of which the acts of January 2d and

February 27th, 1813, were passed. Now, it will at once be seen, that whatever proved to be the actual amount of the duties to which Mr. Gallatin referred, it must necessarily have formed a part of the $11,442,065 34 collected as duties in the years 1813 and 1814; when, at the same time, Mr. Whittlesey has added them together and thus swollen the whole amount to more than $16,000,000.

And let it be observed, too, that we had during three years, not only a lawful commerce with the nations of the world, other than Great Britain, but that the act of Congress of the 9th of April, 1814, repealed the non-importation acts, so far as to permit direct trade with Great Britain in neutral vessels, and also to admit British productions and manufactures when imported from other countries in American as well as neutral vessels. Yet we have seen that the First Comptroller of the Treasury, in estimating the amount received for duties by way of reservations in cases of remissions, has, besides his error of calculation already shown, actually taken into the account the duties accruing from all this legal commerce.

After furnishing us with these extraordinary statements, the Comptroller remarks as follows: "How much of this sum was paid in the character of duties after the goods were seized *pro forma*, as mentioned above, I cannot ascertain, but the petitioner bases his claim on the asserted fact that all importations in 1813 and 1814 were unlawful, and that no legal duties could have been collected, as the importations or introductions were in violation of the non-importation acts then in force." I feel compelled to pronounce this an entire fabrication. *When, where,* or *how,* have I based my claim upon the ground above stated, or even uttered a single sentence from which such an idea could be inferred?

In conclusion, I have only to add, that, with such errors of fact, and such ignorance of law, as have been exhibited by Comptroller Whittlesey, I feel persuaded that Congress will give no weight whatever to his report, in the consideration and decision of my case.

I have the honor to remain,
Respectfully, your ob't serv't,

C P. VAN NESS.

www.ingramcontent.com/pod-product-compliance
Lightning Source LLC
LaVergne TN
LVHW020742120826
845150LV00010B/2353

* 9 7 8 1 4 1 8 1 9 4 2 3 9 *